COACHING KIDS
- ALL TEAM SPORTS -

To an old & dear friend - Don Pardubsky

Frank (Duke) Watts

Frank (Duke) Watts

Published by EC3 Corp
Grand County Colorado U.S.A.
P. O. Box 205
Winter Park, CO 80482

Library of Congress Control Number: 2006924009

ISBN 13: 978-0-9765492-1-5
ISBN 10: 0-9765492-1-2

Printed in the United States of America

Published in the United States of America by:
EC3 Corp
Grand County, Colorado
www.ecm5tools.com
ec3corp@rkymtnhi.com

First Edition: May 2007

Sports

Disclaimer

Should any improvement take place in your coaching skills, league administrative skills, or should kids benefit from the techniques here-in, the author and the publisher will take full responsibility. The author and publisher deny all blame but accept all praise. Should the author have misquoted or failed to give proper credit he cannot be held responsible because of his memory - which is excellent, but very short.

Acknowledgement / Dedication

Inspiration for this book comes primarily from the kids and parents who so graciously put up with my blunders as I learned to coach. My thanks must also include my own kids Jenna, Robert, Bill and wife Jane who likewise suffered.

Table of Contents

Introduction

Have you ever:

- Heard a coach hollering at his kids in anger; **"Play Ball"** and wondered what that meant?

- Coached a kid's team against the league organizer who "just happened" to have more talented kids on his team?

- Heard a parent lament that, "Sports shouldn't be so competitive"?

- Been asked by the Recreation District to sign a pledge to "stay out of the process"?

- Seen bottom performers forced off their team?

- Witnessed a parent hollering obscenities at the coach or official?

- Witnessed a coach that tolerated his kids swearing on the field?

- Seen the parents malign the coach?

- Heard the coach malign the parents?

- And on the bright side, had a kid smile at you in the grocery store and say, "Hi Coach"?

Well I have! These typical problems (except the last, of course) sound like we have some bad people in the process. By my experience, it usually isn't the people, it's the process.

Much has been written about coaching kids. Most books are sport specific – covering only one sport. They go into considerable depth on that sport. Certainly, if you're going to coach any sport, you should find and read a book on that sport. One that is applicable to young kids.

Some other books are general - mostly feel-good psychological stuff. They often focus on how to make the participants feel better – not necessarily perform better. Feel better as in sports where there are no winners or losers. Just like in . . .ah . . . ah . . . well . . . there must be some sport where there are no winners or losers! You will find little written, however, related directly to the basic challenge of coaching kids of young ages, regardless of the sport. And less on organizing kid sports from the coach and league viewpoints.

I will draw heavily on my own experience; playing sports, coaching and outhouse-tipping. Outhouse tipping was a team sport although not too modern. Using "biffy-tipping" will allow me to be generic – to use that analogy instead of listing many specific team sports or saying "all team sports over and over - baseball, basketball field hockey, football, flag-football, ice hockey, lacrosse, rugby, soccer, softball, tee-ball, track, volleyball and whatever team sport I have missed. **I will use this technique in order to treat this subject in a general way and with a little humor – as little as you will find anywhere! It will also be my way of not "favoring" any one team sport over another, or all others.**

This book will address coaching and organizing K through middle school, covering the basics of coaching which are applicable to any team sport. Coaching high school kids is generally an outhouse of a different color.

This book is about coaching kids at a very impressionable stage of life. A stage when they will learn to love the sport or not, play it well or not, to appreciate competition or not, to become a fan or not, or to progress to the next level or not.

I will also look closely at the league organization and its duties. An aspect often ignored. I will tend to be very dogmatic about what should or should not be done. You will need to keep in mind that there are exceptions to all rules. Writing about the possible exceptions would make this work longer and dilute the message. Thus little time will be spent writing about exceptions.

Also remember, my "rules' are based on mistakes that I have made - not necessarily the best approach to learning to coach or writing about coaching kids. So now you may be wondering just what does qualifies me, a mistake making, grumpy old biffy-tipper to write about coaching kids.

As many others, I have played many summer and winter sports in the "sand lots". I've played many different organized sports. Have a couple of high school letters. Have shared in the raising of three kids. Coached several different team sports for twenty-six kid-seasons. Taught skiing to disabled kids for five seasons. Discussed coaching at some length with other coaches and observed many paid and volunteer coaches at work, and loved almost every minute of it.

As mentioned before, I know most of the team sports well but I'm *not* qualified to tell you how to coach. This coach is only able to tell you how to avoid mistakes when coaching kids - because I have been there and done that, just about as well as the worst. I have arguably made more mistakes than any other volunteer coach in modern history. **You can certainly do better.**

Chapter 1
Sports, Love and Lament

Kid sports represent what's best about America. Sports offer physical fitness while having fun. Sports offer fun for participants and their families, an established set of rules, instant reward for most who participate, and usually instant consequences for those who break the rules. Sports offer the excitement of competition as an individual and with a team. They offer an opportunity to excel. Team sports teach kids practical lessons in teamwork, learning how to win and learning how to act after you win or loose. **Learning how to lead, follow or get out of the way.** Sports offer a cleansing of the mind from school, work or family pressures. There is typically a clear outcome – little fuzziness. (You either tip the outhouse or you don't.) There is a kinship found in sports that is often lacking in many other endeavors. Many characteristics of sports are and should be prevalent in other life pursuits.

Yes, sports have a dark side. Some college and pro athletes are the worst of role models. Some end up in jail or dead. The news media folks have a fixation about reporting such events. They seldom put those acts in perspective, however. What percentage of our pro or college athletes do such things? Even in the pro ranks, where money does tend to corrupt, it is very small. But that isn't the impression you would get watching the evening news. Unfortunately, this is the image some parents have. You and I can't do much about the news media except complain – the same as with umpires. We can also show kids a good role model and teach them what teamwork means.

As Terry Frei wrote in *Third Down and a War To Go*, **"Done right, sports teach. Sports bond. Sports enrich. Sports are about lessons and unbreakable friendships that can last through one man's lifetime. And Longer."**

At dinner the other evening a friend commented that the sand-lots are empty! Where did the kids go? How often do you see kids playing in an empty lot, field or greenbelt? Kids organizing the contest as they choose, playing a game without adults, learning how to get along with their peers? Are all the kids at home watching TV?

Biffy-tippers often just chose sides and played without coaches, officials or direct supervision. Did it hurt our self-esteem to be chosen last? Sure, but we got over it and that taught us one of life's hard lessons - we are all good and bad at something and finding our strengths and weaknesses is part of life. In elementary school, a couple of teachers were usually on the playground, but they were just there to settle arguments. That is, if they could get to us before a fight broke out. Yes, we had fights on occasion. It didn't seem to hurt us. Good preparation for the boxing team. Probably those fights worked off some of the frustration that today might lead to some kid bringing a gun or knife to school.

We usually learned how to settle our problems without fighting. I especially remember the tackle football games in grade school. Yes – tackle – *in grade school!* Without pads or helmets! Can you imagine that happening in a modern school? We spent hours and hours on a field, on the ice, at the back yard hoop with no supervision. We traded, negotiated, bartered, blackmailed and threatened (to take the ball and go home). But we played, talked "outhouse drivel" and most of all, had fun.

Perhaps we should still let the kids do their own thing, as we once did. But most parent(s) are working and no one is home to keep one eye on the sandlot. So for better or worse, adults have organized sports, structured them and turned them into a highly programmed activity. So now we need to figure out how to make kids sports the best possible experience for all involved.

Nothing like a
Solid connection.

Chapter 2
Competition

We were competitive. Most of us wanted to win, no matter what the game. There was nothing wrong with competition. Today is no different in that regard. Boys especially, are naturally competitive. In fact, as girl's sports have emerged, they are also very competitive. But I digress.

Should youth sports be competitive? Yes. But do we need to be so adult driven? At what age should kids be organized and coached by adults? Can we return to the sand lot? Maybe if one parent is home when the kids aren't in school - one parent who knows where the kids are at all times. Maybe when outhouses make a comeback! So what then? The best current choice is an association of volunteer parents to organize, coach and assist the coach. Or a school or recreation district which will involve the parents in a meaningful fashion.

Can we combine the best of the sand-lot with organized youth sports? Can or should a competitive sport culture be kept out of organized youth sports? Should there be a clear separation of "Competitive Leagues" and "Non-competitive Leagues?" Can we combine the best of the sandlot, organization and competition? Can the non-competitive league just not keep score? Will the kids, parents and coaches on both sides feel like winners?

This book won't answer all these questions but it will make you think about what is best for the kids. **Not what is best for** the parents, not best for the teachers, not best for the city, not best for the recreation district, not best for the coaches, not best for the administrators, not best for the school board but what is best for the kids.

Chapter 3
Paid Coaches or Volunteer Parents?

Who should coach kids? The short answer is; anyone who is interested in helping kids learn to play a sport and have fun at it. To be considered effective by the kids and parents, however, is a separate challenge.

Since early days of outhouse tipping, kid-coaching has been a challenge equal to finding an outdoor biffy in a snowstorm. Because of this challenge, some folks think that professional coaches should be hired to coach kids. They say that kid's sports should be left up to the Recreation District (read Government) and they should hire the coaches - someone with a recreation degree. Get "real pros" who know what they are doing. Parents should take a pledge to stay out of the process. This is the modern trend. Other folks think that parents should organize and coach kid sports. I would favor parents doing the organizing and coaching for reasons that will become apparent.

Coach may be a parent, teacher or a recreation district professional. Whether done by paid or volunteer coaches, however, the parents must not be left out of the process. Parents often know the sport as well as anyone. They know kids better. They have a vested interest in the process and the outcome. There is nothing taught in college that trumps a parent's knowledge of kids.

On occasion, problem parents need to be purged from the organization. When the government is in control, they find it very difficult to purge troublemakers. Thus, they ask all parents to take a pledge to stay out of the process. A few parents do turn out to be serious troublemakers. How can the government tell a taxpayer to take a hike? They can't, and don't. Also, parents are free. No taxes needed to pay coaches. For all these reasons, parents organizing and coaching a kid's team sport is generally better than using professionals.

The paid coach generally thinks that they have to do it alone. After all, isn't that what they are paid for? They therefore exclude parents. Sometimes the recreation district will adopt the paid coach approach. They typically ask parents to sign a pledge to "keep out of it". This is exactly the wrong approach!

The paid coach wants a paid assistant, then paid mileage, trips for "training", seminars for "improvement", on ad-nausea. Then the organization will need more money to throw at "the problems". Often, the very problems created by excluding parents.

Don't believe the mantra that "parents are different now". They "don't want to be involved" or "they don't have time to be involved". Parents are no different now than ever. Their kids are usually number-one in their hearts and minds. They want to see their kids get the best teaching and training available. They want to see them succeed. They generally want to be involved in their kid's sport. They will find the time.

Who needs the government to coach kid sports anyway? Probably those parents who want someone to baby sit their kid. Should we pay taxes to make youth sports a babysitting service? The few who don't want to be involved should hire baby sitter - not dump their kid on a coach. An association of parents with parents coaching is the better choice in my opinion.

Volunteer parents should be used to coach, officiate, organize and administrate. Parents should coach the kids and organize the program while the government should furnish the field, rink, park, court, outhouses and pledge to stay out of the process. The parents lead, the kids follow and the government gets out of the way.

Having said that, I recognize that paid coaches may be here to stay in some communities. The paid coach should still involve the parents, whether they work for a recreation district or a school. The paid coach and their organization should still follow the "outhouse rules".

Volunteers or paid, realize that some days, nothing works.

Some days—
Nothing Works!

Chapter 4
Can You Coach Kids?

So you think you can coach kids. You know you can. After all, you have played the game - perhaps excelled at the game. You know the rules. You have studied the fine points. Watched the pros and understand the strategy. All this qualifies you to be a semi-failure when coaching kids. Lots of kid-coaches have those qualifications. Lots of us have been partial failures in our first season or two. For example, knowing your sport too well, may cause you to make your teaching too complex.

I'm talking here about the very formative years - elementary and middle school. With those young kids we need to keep it simple. Example; when biffy tipping, if you are short, stay on the side of the outhouse so you don't fall in the hole.

In fact, if you're a real student of the sport – make it your hobby – then your chances of failure with young kids may be more likely than the next coach. You can probably lose them before your first practice is over, instead of somewhere around the third game as I did.

Using a baseball example; at earlier ages, with someone on first and a ground ball is hit to the infield, forget the double play. Keep it simple – make the throw to first and get the easy out. As they get older, teach them to cut down the lead runner. Then, at later ages, go for the double play. At exactly what age, depends upon the talent available.

Now don't burn this book and call the league to tell them to forget it. Of course you can coach. You will do a much better job than I did. You will probably learn more than the kids will. It will likely be more rewarding for you than for the kids.

Coach's first priority must be to help them to enjoy the game. If they are having fun, they will learn easily. If instructions or expectations are too complex, it will be difficult for you and them to have fun.

Have just enough doubt about your kid-coaching ability to finish this book. Maybe you can learn from this biffy-tipper's four hundred and seventy-two mistakes. I'm well qualified to tell you how to make mistakes when coaching kids. Please do not panic, however, I will not cover all four hundred and seventy-two mistakes. Can't even remember them all! I have, however, made some (or seen some made) over and over and remember those well. I will also frequently slip into my outhouse-ego and tell you how to do it "right".

Let's ask again. Can you coach kids? Of course you can. **What you choose to teach them, how much you teach them, how much fun they have, how much they like the sport, how happy the parents are, how much you win; all may be an outhouse of a different color.**

Chapter 5
Clear and Simple

Start by figuring out why outhouses for young families had a little step and a small hole in the bench next to the big one. Realize that all the kids may not understand the terms used. You cannot assume anything.

When coaching tee-ball, I spent a lot of practice time batting, catching ground balls and throwing to first. When the first game rolled around, one of my boys got wood on the ball – his first in a game. We hollered RUN, RUN, RUN! He did – **directly to third base.** I had neglected to cover base running. What do they say about how to spell "assume?"

As an assistant coach for a kid's basketball team, I was telling the kids that they have to rebound under both baskets - to fight harder for rebounds. One kid, listening intently, asked, "Coach, what's a rebound?" And he wasn't the only kid who didn't understand what a rebound is. Now ask yourself, what will happen when the coach, not having defined and demonstrated a rebound, goes on to explain that defensive rebounds must be "cleared to the outside for a fast break in transition"? **Instructions need to be simple, clear and demonstrated, demonstrated and demonstrated.**

As a hockey coach, I told the kids to keep their stick on the ice. This is for safety, because that is where the puck is and because it is the best position for reaction to most any situation. As we talked, one kid held his stick waist high. I looked at him and said, "Stick on the ice!" He looked around and did nothing. I pointed at him and said, more loudly, "Stick on the ice!" **He finally dropped his stick on the ice.** After an embarrassing moment, I showed them the best position for almost all situations is to keep the <u>blade</u> of the stick on the ice, knees bent and head up. Set up examples to demonstrate, in action, what you mean.

C'mon _ _ _ _ Play Football !!!!

The ultimate bad example was a football coach I saw and heard screaming to his kids during a game; "PLAY FOOTBALL!" The veins stood out on his neck. He screamed it many times. "PLAY FOOTBALL!" It was certainly simple enough but not very clear. They thought that's what they were doing. It's like hollering my dog's name at my dog. "BLUE! BLUE! BLUE!" The dog glances at me and says to himself, "Yep, that's my name, do you want me to sit, stay, come, lie down, fetch or what?"

When the coach hollers "play football", what happens? The kids that were doing something right probably decided that they were doing it wrong. Those doing something wrong didn't know it and "play football" wasn't helping any of them. If all the coach can think of is gross generalizations like "play football", he or she should keep their mouth shut. Wasn't it Abraham Lincoln that said, "Better to keep my mouth shut and be thought a fool, than to open it and remove all doubt."

Maybe you have some time or schedule limitations and want a partner to co-coach. This biffy-tipper co-coached a girls softball team and a boys coach-pitch baseball. (coach pitched under-hand to his / her own team). We were very successful. This can work, but you have to put a little extra attention into coordinating the job and the co-coach should also be a parent. Co-coaching a boy's baseball team, I remember telling the kids to put their glove on their knee when in the defensive-ready position. The co-coach Jerry had already told them not to put their glove on their knee but to have it ready by the knee. We had them fully confused! Before the pitch we'd call to them to "be ready guys".

They would go through something that looked like a Saint-Vitas-Dance while they were glancing back and forth between us. We had both missed the point. Either method would be OK. Neither of us hit the important points except by implication - keep your feet apart, knees bent, glove on or near your knee and watch the ball / batter - not us.

Co-coaching does have definite advantages. If something goes wrong, you can always blame the other guy. If a kid isn't called about a practice or a schedule change, you can always blame the other guy. Also, if you are coaching alone, the team tends to take on your personality. You may be surprised by what you see. You might not even like what you see or hear. One year, in about the second game, I looked around and saw my kids constantly telling each other what they were doing wrong. They were great critics. Listening carefully, I heard my own words coming from their mouths. If I'd had a co-coach, I could have blamed him or her. **One encouragement is better than three critiques.**

In general, you should take on the team alone. Don't share the responsibility and run the risk of confusing the kids and the parents. This doesn't mean that you do it all alone. **It does mean that the buck stops with one person – the coach.**

Think about your coaches when you were growing up. What did they do that you liked, was most fun and kept you thinking. Do read a book about coaching your sport. Try to find a book that is directed at kids. Failing that, find a book that is structured so that the basics are separated from the advanced techniques. Look for the basic drills and plays. Weave them into your plan.

Some books are structured from the basics up. Absorb the basics and that part of the "progression" as you see applicable for your age group.

Must coach have played the sport? Preferably yes, but you don't have to be at the semi-pro level in order to coach kids. If the league needs coaches, go for it regardless of your experience. You may do a better job than many with more credentials.

The parents and kids don't expect pro performance from the coach. Man, woman, teen or young adult, the coaching requirements are the same. Kids expect you to make it fun for them. Parents would expect you to teach them some basics in keeping with their age and prior experience. You need to find ways to make practices move quickly, be intense and fun. And you must involve the parents. **You must find a way to relate to them and to have them relate to you - both kids and parents.**

One of my own son's coaches purposely demonstrated the wrong way to do the task. He would laugh at himself and the kids would laugh and go do it right. If they made a mistake on that task in practice he would say "You did that as bad as I do!" I used that general idea when teaching handicapped kids to ski. When they fell, I'd try to fall as quickly as possible, laughing all the way. They would look at me and laugh too. Then I'd tell them, "If you aren't falling, you aren't learning." I learned to ski backwards and to fall from that posture pretty well.

This is not to say that you shouldn't have behavior rules and enforce them. Tough-love if you will. Have a few, well thought out rules. **The number one rule being – "when it's my turn to talk, it's your turn to listen."**

Chapter 6
Behavior

Need I even say that an unwritten rule prohibits smoking, drinking or swearing with the kids around! Intensity doesn't come from swearing - it comes from practices. The kids will reflect your behavior – good or bad.

I just attended a grandson's soccer game. The kids on the opposition were swearing on the field – foul stuff. The swearing was directed at the opposition players. When the coach was called on it, he had an attitude that was indicative of a problem. He must have shrugged and raised his hands – palms up – several times. Meaning "what can I do?" he was also said, "What can I do?" This coach needed only to say to folks that he would have a talk with his team and swearing will not be tolerated. That coach probably couldn't say ten words himself without swearing. **If you don't understand how simple this is, shrug and raise your hands palms up! If you just did that, close this book and don't coach.**

When it comes to the officials making perceived mistakes, let the officials know that you disagree but don't make much of it at the time. If you do, you could be giving your kids an excuse for loosing. Only a tiny fraction of games are so close that an official call(s) will affect the result. If you are loud and overbearing about it, the official may be looking closer than ever to find your teams transgressions. Think about it, it is just human nature. Take serious complaints to the association and the other complaints to the outhouse.

At these young ages you will typically be coaching your own kid(s). Coaching your own kids, especially boys, is very difficult. Kids don't take coaching from Mom or Dad very well. Also we may not be as patient with our own child. What should you do - put them on a different team? Double the number of trips and hours involved? I heard this seriously suggested on a radio show. No, just sit down with your assistants and make a deal. No coach will tell his own kid what to do or not to do or how to do it. **Each coach will approach one of the other coaches and ask them to tell their kid what to do.**

Trust the old outhouse tipper on this one – they will listen much better to the other coach. In fact, after practice your kid is likely to tell you exactly what the other coach said – like you didn't know. Just say, "Oh yeah, that sounds like a good idea to me!"

Chapter 7
The Organized Coach

The days of the sand lot have gone the way of the stay-at-home parent. Since it currently seems to be the only practical alternative - coach and organizers, get organized. Let's do it in a way that is best for the kids.

There are two different levels of issues in kid's sports - organization issues and coaching issues. Organization issues include how to divide the kids, what facilities will be used, who will coach, what rules will be used and the schedule for practices and games. These are issues for the parent association or the government entity. Then, execution of the plan, is the coach's job. What exact responsibilities go with the coaches and which with the association? It should be the association's task to make that division of responsibilities very clear. We will get to the association later, for now let's stick with the coach.

How do you get organized for effective outhouse tipping? First, you should attend the pre-season coaches meeting. You will get a roster, a place to practice and a game schedule, or at least know when they will be available. This will be a good time to ask a lot of questions about later organizing subjects. Also attend any coach's clinics available.

First practice(S), find out, as best you can, which kid belongs at each position. This sometimes takes more time than you might want to spend, but it pays off in the long run. Our son was chosen for an all star baseball team to play other similar teams in the post season. His coach spent one and a half hours, the entire first practice time, experimenting with every kid at third base. He also experimented at the same time with all the kids at first base. Hit the ball to third, watch the fielding and the throw to first, the catch at first. Hit the ball to third, watch the fielding and the throw to first, on ad-nausea. The rest of the kids were running bases. He was trying each kid at those two positions. It seemed like a very slow start. It was however, the most well spent practice of all. At that age, the kids tended to pull the ball down third. The kid he chose was little for his age but he was like a vacuum and had a great arm. The kid he put at first had an inaccurate throw but he was big and could catch most anything thrown toward him. He thus filled the two most important positions and learned enough about all the kids to fill the other positions.

In the in-house league, you may not have as much time to properly position kids. Also the league may well have rules about rotating kids in various positions. At very young ages, it may be desirable to have such rotation rules.

It doesn't hurt to ask the kids where they want to play providing you preface it with; "I may not play anybody where they want to." Be especially cautious with your own kid. If you put him at quarterback without trying anyone else at that position you will rightfully open yourself up for criticism. You have an important balancing act to perform. Experiment with kids at different positions. If they don't have confidence in your choices, something will be lacking. If they feel they had a chance, they will perform better wherever you put them.

You need to fully understand the league rules. Know how and when to substitute correctly. Timeouts, fouls/infractions, what is/isn't allowed. Put bluntly, to "take advantage" of every rule. My first year in girl's softball, we knew that stealing bases was allowed after the ball had crossed the plate. We worked on steals to second, third and home. We were the only team that had worked on this and therefore had a considerable advantage. The other coaches were so upset with us (they should have been upset with themselves) that the next year they got the league to eliminate base-stealing. We still won, but I digress.

In short, you can blunder along or **get organized.**

Getting organized
Pays Off !

Chapter 8
Involve the Parents

You can't do a very good job of tipping outhouses by yourself. Even if you do, it isn't much fun. Get the parents involved. **Make it clear when you volunteer that you are going to reserve the right to veto any kid because his parents won't get involved.** If the parent doesn't help, the kid is out. Square that with the association. You will see later that even the single parent with two jobs can help.

At your first team meeting with the kids and at least one parent, outline the league rules and your own rules. One of your rules should be that at least one parent from each family must be involved in the team. Getting the parents involved will mitigate most of the finger-pointing and the frustration that goes with coaching kids. When a parent is involved, it becomes "their team", not "your team". They will look at you differently and you will look at them differently. It took me a few kid-seasons to recognize this fact, and it is a fact. **For those of you who don't believe in facts, if you believe that everything is just a matter of feeling, close this book and go jump into the nearest outhouse hole.**

The total lack of involvement is the soccer coach who asked his parents to be on the other side of the field from him and the kids. Not only not involved, but separated by a playing field. That coach probably didn't want to hear what the parents had to say.

OK, you do see the wisdom of getting parents involved. But what can they do? If you have fifteen kids on a team, that's a lot of parents. Yep, one parent involved for each kid makes fifteen parents, at least according to the old math. Here is the outhouse method to productively involve them all:

- **Coach**
  You are coaching your own kid, so that is one guaranteed parent involved.

- **Assistant Coaches**
  Call for **two assistant coaches.** Outline the job as you see it. Assistants are expected to be at all practices and games. Since emergencies do arise, this will assure that two of the three coaches are at every game and practice. You will need to figure out how to make their time productive - more on that later.

- **Bench Coach**
  Someone dedicated to keep order on the bench. Must be at all games and scrimmages or arrange for a substitute among the parents. This is for safety's sake, especially in games with a bat, stick or a helmet made like a rock. You would appreciate the need for this person if you had seen the kid who was hit with a bat at my grandson's baseball game. This assistant keeps the kids in outhouse tipping order, substitution order and safe. Also he or she gets positive chatter from the bench.

- **Scorekeeper**
  Keeps the score-book and tracks the playing-time. Warns you when a player hasn't been in the game the required or

committed amount of time, or does the substitutions on a prearranged schedule. Monitors the opposition to ensure that they follow the playing time rules.

- **Equipment Manager**
  Someone to pickup all the equipment and bring it to the next practice or game. Or sees to it that all the equipment is accounted for and gets in and out of your vehicle.

- **Telephone Team Manager**
  "Don't call me (the coach), we will call you." If the weather looks poor, don't call me, **we will call you.** Coach makes **one** phone call for a schedule change, practice change or whatever – to the telephone team manager. The telephone manager divides the roster among the telephone team. The leader can also send an email but **don't rely on emails alone** as some folks won't see the email until it's too late. And the telephone is more personal and covers those without email.

- **Telephone Team**
  Three or four parents are needed here. The roster is divided up among them. The telephone team manager calls each one and tells them about the change. They, in turn, call their portion of the kids on the roster – about four calls each. This is a great job for the single parent who has two jobs already.

- **Treat Leader**
  Someone to assure that a treat is there after each game. Nothing fancy – put a dollar limit on it if you wish. "Less is more" especially if you're near meal time. The treat leader

sets up a different parent for each game and or practice. This leader makes sure that all parents participate.

- **Parent-Couple**
  A man and wife (or woman and husband) to make sure that every kid is picked up from all practices and games. They will be the last to leave. They will commit to calling the parents of any kid left standing - to insure the kid and a parent make contact. Also to protect the kids from predators and to protect the coach from false allegations.

- **Publicity Guru**
  Get the team name and kid's names into the local paper or on the radio. Or simply make up a team newsletter for distribution on occasion - at least once at the end of the year. This is a real keepsake - at least for this coach. This person also organizes the end of year party if you wish one.

This is **not coaching by committee.** You and your assistants are the core outhouse tipping teachers. You will still make all the critical decisions but you will get lots of friendly input and support from the parents.

Do not fall into the trap that says "times are different now and the outhouse-method won't work." Some things never change and most parents' attitude toward their kid is and will ever be - unchanged. They will be pleased to be involved. If they won't be involved, they are looking for a baby-sitting service and should be banned from the outhouse. Yes, some single parents with two jobs may need a break. But can't they make three or four phone calls on occasion?

Need all help come only from the parents? No, especially if there is a special older kid who will help. A Middle School or High School kid can make a marvelous assistant coach. A coach with limited experience should look for such a young person to demonstrate and help. Such a person can serve as a great roll model for your kids. One older brother or sister might volunteer instead of a parent. An older sibling or a neighborhood kid could be the head coach providing they properly involve the parents.

Chapter 9
Parent-Kid Meeting

Call one meeting before practices start, or at least at the first practice - right after the coaches meeting - a team meeting (all the kids) **and require at least one parent for each child to attend.** Personally telephone each family. Make it clear that it is a requirement, if one parent isn't there, the kid doesn't play on your team. Make sure that you don't make an exception for the star player(s).

Make a roster before the parent-kid meeting. Make sure that it is put in the hands of each family. Copy the league rules and write down and copy your rules for each family. Give them all a copy of the game schedule when available. Make a copy of your practice schedule for each. Don't rely on every family having a computer or using it – go with hard copy – it eliminates excuses.

Read them your list of jobs. Ask for questions. Discuss each job as necessary. Then ask for volunteers. **You may have to say that the meeting isn't going forward until you have one parent from each family to help.** Say again that you aren't going to do it alone. Outline the jobs without volunteers and wait. Sometimes there will be a long pause before they start to volunteer. Don't give them any choice. My way – parents helping – or the highway.

Make sure you are prepared and that you **keep the parent meeting short.** I've seen the most meaningless bunch of outhouse drivel put out at such meetings. Our daughter signed up for a competitive hockey team. The parent-kid meeting was a disaster. Nothing was written down or handed out. Lasted over two hours. Coffee and cake and no substance. A lot of talk about how expensive ice-time is - which is a fact. No talk about minimum playing time rules. It turned out that there were none. There were too many girls carried on the team. Our daughter was quite capable, so she had a reasonable amount of playing time but there were many unhappy parents because of little or no playing time for their kid. Except for that meeting, there was zero parent involvement.

It also turned out that the co-coaches (wouldn't you guess) not only hadn't played the game at any level, but they could barely skate and had never tipped an outhouse. It slowly developed that one of their daughters was the superstar and the phantom coach. Practices were nearly a farce. Our daughter didn't learn two new things all season. They did have some very good talent besides the superstar. It was proof that talent can substitute for coaching - they won the Minnesota State Championship that year for their age group.

Some called it a wonderful season, those parents whose kids didn't get much playing time were very unhappy. I thought much of it was a sham. It was purposely designed to get money from the parents whose girls weren't going to play much in order to pay for ice time and tournament fees.

You must make it clear to the parents that you have a life too. You are not a taxi service. If parents want to get together to ride-share that is something they can do on their own. If they have doubts about the practice because of the weather - they should just show up - unless they get a call from the telephone committee.

Make it clear to the kids and parents that you do recognize that the art of coaching is, like outhouse tipping, not an exact science. You will make mistakes. If a parent wishes to suggest or complain they must do it in private, one on one with the coach, calmly and quietly.

You should reserve the right to decide whether or not a kid continues to play for the team based upon the parents co-operation and behavior. Yes, behave as a parent should, or you and your kid will not be on our team. The association must back you in this requirement.

When it comes to playing time – a very important issue to most parents – you can give them an evasive answer like you hear politicians give to tough questions. Or you can use outhouse logic to tell them you will make every effort to make sure that you meet and exceed the league rules about playing time and that you will have help from the scorer/timekeeper to assure same. If a team consists of kids from a couple of ages, say 7 and 8 year olds, let the parents and kids know that the older kids will usually get longer playing time. Next year the younger kids will be the "old folks". Also, tell the "old folks" that because they are a year older, it doesn't guarantee more playing time. They will need to hustle to get it. The better their cooperation, participation, practice attendance and attitude the more playing time they may get.

If the league doesn't have rules about playing time, they are poorly organized and there will be lots of coaches and parents locked in the outhouse - more on that later. In the meantime, think through the issue and devise a meaningful and fair personal rule. Do some calculating - total minutes, innings, periods, total number of kid-minutes, innings, periods, number of outhouses to be tipped, etc. What is a reasonable minimum time to commit realizing that you want to win, <u>but not at all cost.</u>

Winning isn't everything – it's the only thing!

Chapter 10
Win At All Costs?

At young ages, the primary difference in the "win at all cost" coach and other coaches is in the treatment of the kids on the bottom of the totem pole. **The win at all cost coach can be spotted because they find a way to drive off the bottom performers.**

The poorest performer or two may be singled out. They may be ridiculed in front of the rest of the team. When schedule changes occur, they don't get the word. During scrimmages, they almost always sit down at the start. They never start a game. Everyone on the team is called by their first name, except them. I'm sure I've left out some of the "better" techniques. I've asked coaches why they didn't have the same number of kids that I had. The answer is often that a couple of kids quit because "they really didn't want to play this sport." Sure, and outhouses tip by themselves.

Many of us revere Green Bay Packer coach and multiple Super Bowl winner Vince Lombardi, who said, "Winning isn't everything – it's the only thing!" I agree, as long as we are talking about pro sports. **But this ain't about pro sports, it's about kids sports.**

Most coaches want to win - but put it in perspective. Bill Koch, a US Cross Country champion and Olympic medal winner said "Winning isn't everything in sports, striving for excellence is!" It was Grantland Rice who so wisely wrote:

> **For when the one Great Scorer comes,**
> **To write against your name,**
> **He marks - not that you won or lost,**
> **But how you played the game.**

Let the parents and kids know you like to win. You will not apologize for a win. You will be proud to win. But it will not be a season of winning at all costs.

You will also, reluctantly, teach them to loose graciously. The other team played very well. On this day, they were the better biffy-tipping team. The more good things you say about the opponents that just beat you, the easier that makes the loss. Describe those things the opposition did very well. We can still be proud. We can still have fun. We will get them next time.

Don't ever blame the officials for a loss in front of your kids. Bad calls seldom make a difference in winning or losing. If you think there is a problem with a particular game / official, take it to the organization leadership.

All too often, one team has been "stacked" by the chief organizer, who also coaches. Their team just happens to get more talent. Sure, and your outhouse was tipped by the wind. If you get into a season before realizing this was done, tough it out and insist that the methods of choosing teams must change next season. In this circumstance, I would not hesitate to tell the parents what has happened.

Keep a playing time record for your own team and perhaps the opposition. It can be used to show a disgruntled parent. If you suspect that another coach is not following the playing time rules bring it to the league officials to find out if they will monitor that team. If you see them again in the schedule, have your scorekeeper / timer track their playing time as well as your own. Take the opposing coach aside with your timekeeper and explain what you see happening. If necessary, take the results to the league officials.

Chapter 11
Protect the Kids and Yourself

Much has been said and written about the rare abuse of kids who are participating in sports. Most "solutions" favor some form of "screening".

I read that *The Little League* will require sex offender background checks for every manager, coach and volunteer who routinely deals with players (*US News*, 21 Oct 02). Now there is a decision from a bunch of folks who have never tipped an outhouse. What will the affect be? It will discourage volunteers. We want all the parents involved, shall we put them all thru the background checks? It will be very costly. Who wants to go through the hassle? It will have exactly the wrong affect. It will discourage involvement of parents.

Oh, and by the way, all you perverts – make sure you go register with the police so this can work! Folks that make such rules are like an outhouse without a hole in the bench. Want to bet that these "decision makers" are paid employees who have spent too much time in an indoor toilet?

I listened to a radio talk show where folks were talking about how to prevent perverts from getting at your kids via coaching. Require coaches to be screened by the city cops. Access the state crime data base. Require psychological testing. Call in the FBI. Callers went on and on about elaborate methods of identifying pedophiles, screening, taking lie detector tests, etc. It was obviously being discussed with the assumption that the coach was alone in the job.

How about false accusations? How can we prevent a coach from being falsely accused of abusing the kids in any fashion? Can "screening prevent that?

The simple, direct and low cost approach is to get the parents involved. The parent involvement alone will discourage the twisted ones. The "Parent-Couple" is built-in protection for the kids and for the coach. They must attend as a couple at all practices and games. They are the last to leave. They assure that each kid has been picked up by a parent. The league should require this. The coach should, even if the league doesn't. It's good self protection. What's to be complicated here? Get the parents involved.

Since the parent-couple approach requires a considerable time, a rotation of the couple may be needed. Have one set of parents coordinate this. It is a lot better than forcing every parent through some kind of background check of questionable benefit.

Having said all of that, the league running the head coaches by the national pedophile data base is good protection for everyone – but not by itself.

Chapter 12
Intensity

Back in the early 50s, a great Russian coach by the name of Anatol Tarasov took charge of Russia's National Hockey Team. Before he retired in 1972, he had four Olympic Gold Medals and twelve World Championships. Experts all over the world acclaimed Anatol as the greatest coach the game had ever known! Canadian and American hockey people often claimed that the key to the Russian hockey success was the length of their season and the quantity of training time. Anatol responded that it was rather the "tempo and the intensity" of each practice. His theory was "train hard and briskly or don't train at all." Coach Herb Brooks used the same technique to coach the "Miracle On Ice" Olympic Hockey Team.

Practices

Generally, the challenge is not to get them "up for games", it is rather just the opposite. Practices need to be more intense than is generally thought. Coach is often a nice guy in practices. Casual, joking and easy going. Come game time however the coach sounds like he is in an outhouse that was tipped on its door. You need to find ways to get them "up" for practices and, sometimes, to settle them down for games.

When I started coaching, I expected to have leisurely practices knowing that the kids would "step it up" in the games. I was wrong! Your practices need to be intense. I'm talking here about the coach and the drills. At game time you (the coach) need to be less intense. Still intense but less vocal may be a better way to say it. Coach needs to be, in word and action, at a high pitch in practice drills. Then, come game time, tone down your voice and actions. The kids know that a game is going on and it means more than practices, you don't have to tell that even to young kids.

The team will start to form habits at practices. It is a fact of nature that humans are largely a creature of habit. Help them to form good basic practice habits and to do them intensely.

Kids have a short attention span so don't have long practices. **A one hour of high tempo practice is worth three hours of the other kind.** Certainly, make practices no longer than an hour or hour and a half including a scrimmage. Use available practice time wisely. Write down a plan for each practice.

Don't stop practicing when the game-schedule starts. There is a reason for that old adage – "Practicing tipping outhouses, makes perfect outhouse tipping." This saying was since shortened somewhat, but I digress.

Any team can tip an outhouse but it takes intensity to tip a four-holer in eight nanoseconds. Intensity (or tempo or concentration) at your practices will, to a great extent, determine the intensity in games. It's that "extra something" you hear coaches talk about. It is often responsible for the "momentum" you hear announcers talk about.

Ask for a kid to volunteer to show the others how it is done. Don't always pick the same kid. Spread the glory around. When a kid is picked to demonstrate, they rightly think "the coach thinks I'm good." That is exactly how you want every kid on the team to feel. Spreading the glory is important to the kids having fun - and to winning.

Watch for places in your practice where the kids are standing around. Work out a drill for those in line. Have an assistant coach run that drill. Never assume that they know the basics. High standards, high expectations, high humor and high practice intensity will produce the best results.

Scrimmages

End your practice with a scrimmage. Have an assistant coach(s) be the official during scrimmages. **Follow the same rules in scrimmages that the league will follow during games.** Explain what violation occurred after every whistle. Stop scrimmages for quick coaching pointers. Have the kids stop/freeze when the "official", or you, blow the whistle. This will allow you to give more meaningful tips. Do it quickly and move on.

Catch the kids doing something right and let them know about it - right then. Every time you catch them doing something right, it will reinforce that behavior. During practices and scrimmages highlight any good progress for every kid. Not falsely, but whenever they do something a little better than before. Atta-Boy / Girl! Way to go Bill! Yes Bob, well done! That's great Jenna! This rule also applies to games.

Finish practice/scrimmage with a short talk. Keep such talks very short or you will loose them to the attention span thing. Tell the kids what they need to work on. Ask them to close their eyes and imagine themselves doing the particular move or play. Ask them to work on that move or play at home in the basement, yard and in their minds – visualization does help.

Game Time

During games, there isn't much you can do except to keep your cool and continue teaching. Your teaching should be generally directed at those on the bench or just coming to the bench. You should still display an intensity about your words and actions. You can yell "good stuff" to the kids in the game and minimal instruction. The kids in the game may be too occupied to hear, let alone respond. If you have complicated instructions, a time-out is in order.

Try to have fun and try to keep the kids' intensity up without losing your cool or letting them lose their cool. If a kid does "lose it", it is best to get them out of the game for a little while.

After the game have a quick wrap up meeting. Have the treat coordinator hold the treats until you're finished summing up the good that occurred and what we need to work on. If you lost, praise the other team. Today they were the better team but next time we can be the better team.

Teaching
Concentration...
pays off!

A. Venezia

Chapter 13
Problem Parents

You have heard the same complaints about kid's sports that I have. Many coaches say that the kids aren't a problem, the parents are the problem. Got an email from a good friend which tells the story about that kind of parent:

At one point during a game, the coach called one of his 8-year-old baseball players aside and asked, "Do you understand what co-operation is, what a team is?" The little boy nodded in the affirmative. "Do you understand what matters is that we win or lose together as a team?" The little boy nodded yes. Coach continued, "I'm sure you know, when an out is called, you shouldn't argue, curse, attack the umpire, or call him a lousy bleep. Do you understand all that?" Again the little boy nodded. He continued, "And when I take you out of the game so another boy gets a chance to play, it's bad sportsmanship to call your coach a lousy bleep isn't it?" Again the little boy nodded. "Good," said the coach. "Now go over and explain that to your mother."

Obnoxious behavior from any parent is a rare but serious problem. Let the parents know at the team meeting that loud mouthed criticism of an official or a coach can only hurt the team's chances. Sometimes a one on one with a parent is in order. Probably best to call them on the phone. If you want the other parents to know, then ask (in front of the other parents) the troublesome parent to stay around for a minute. Another technique a fellow coach used was to give the ref a "heads-up" about a troublesome parent. They should have the authority to hold the game until the troublemaker leaves the area.

I had such a lousy parent one year. As you might suspect, his wife had come to the parent-kid meeting. He was obnoxious in the stands to both the officials and to me. I could hear some of it from the bench but the parents later told me details that I didn't hear. I tried to ignore it – a bad decision. It was very divisive for the team and the parents. I made the mistake of not telling him to take a hike.

On occasion, a parent will tend to interfere or try to take over your job. A friend called this type of parent a "helicopter parent" – because they "hover" over you. Take this parent aside and have a short discussion on the matter. Tell them you will recommend them for coaching a team next year, but this year it will be done your way.

If parents refuse to be involved or are trouble makers, they and their kid are off the team. Banished to the outhouse! You need to cover this critical point with the league leadership beforehand. As we will cover later, the league should have a method for purging the troublemakers. Left unchecked, a few parents will create one of those situations we read about in the papers. Don't let it get anywhere close to that – get rid of them.

Few parents are real troublemakers. However, coaches often say that the parents are always complaining - to them, behind their back, to other parents and to the association. The parents say that coach doesn't play my kid enough. He or she is playing favorites. They aren't teaching them much. The schedule was changed and we didn't hear about it. On ad-nausea. What's wrong here? When I question the coach, it usually becomes apparent that the coach is a one man show, or at best has one assistant - who may not even be a parent. The parents aren't involved. They will be super-frustrated and critical when they aren't involved. They have no ownership in the team - they only have ownership in their kid. So what's complicated here? Involve the parents.

Chapter 14
The League

So much for parents and coaches. Let's get to the association leadership. Much can go wrong here - well meaning folks who determine many issues.

There is sometimes an outhouse quandary over a "charter" for the league. A charter statement that points out how important and "feel good" sport or competition should be. I had a friend who told of the endless arguments over the "goal statement" for his league. What a waste of valuable time. But don't we need a goal/charter statement for the organization? Sure, go to the Internet and find a statement you like and adopt it. Nice going – now let's get into the important stuff.

The league needs to have clear cut policies about six issues. The six most important things that the league officials must do (in addition to getting good coaches and training them), in no particular order:

- **A method to purge the troublemakers from a team and the league.**
- **Policy for balancing the playing time.**
- **Policy for balancing the talent.**
- **Managing kid-drop-out.**
- **Determine if a "competitive" and / or a "non-competitive" league(s) is in order.**
- **Obtain facilities, set and publish the schedule early.**

These and other rules should be carefully considered and then written down and given to every coach. They should be given enough copies for every family.

The need for addressing the first issue - purging the trouble-makers - is obvious.

The next three issues are the most important for obtaining "parity" in the league - a condition wherein each team has a roughly equal opportunity to win or loose. In the ideal, each team could win and loose the same number of games. Like the NFL with their draft, salary caps, etc. Parity also optimizes the importance of the coach. An outstanding coach can still win more than "their share".

Competitive, non-competitive or both is a very important decision for the league.

By my experience, the facility selection and scheduling are usually done well, while some or all of the other issues are ignored.

Chapter 15
Purge the Troublemakers

This problem exists in all sports at all levels. A few parents, family or friends (usually a parent) frequently act like a WOFATP (Waste Of Food And Toilet Paper – pronounced wofateepee). **The league needs to have a method, established ahead of time, to purge the troublemaker.** He or she is typically the parent who doesn't help. They just stand back and complain about the coaches, officials or the league.

During my coaching career, I never saw a really effective method of handling the trouble-maker. It came down to the coach saying, "That guy and his kid are out of here or I am." This is a poor position to put a coach in. On a plane trip, I met a coach who told me of a fine method of handling the WOFATP. At least it sounded good to me. The following is roughly what their league did.

The league authorized each coach to warn the troublemaker and required the coach to do it privately . They made a "one-strike-card". The card makes it clear that if it happens again they are off that team. Coach must immediately tell the league when a card is given and explain why. The league then furnished the coach with a two-strikes-card with that person's name on it.

When necessary, the coach gives a two-strikes-card. This card tells the parent that they and their child are no longer part of that team but that he / she can contact the league office to be given one last chance on another team. If that parent wants to try another team they can. If they choose to go to another team, the new team coach is given a "three-strikes-card" with the parent's name on it. If that person acts up again - **"you're out of here!"**

Three strikes and you're out! I love it. Maybe a three-strikes-card system is also needed for coaches who have ignored this book. Coaches who yell obscenities, or let their players yell obscenities at the officials, players, other coaches or worse. You bet your biffy – three strikes and you're out. Perhaps coaches should only be allowed two strikes.

Purging rules should be spelled out in the handouts for the parents. The parent can see or call the league to state their case anytime. Sounds like a fine method to me.

Whether or not you use this particular method, there must be a way of getting rid of the troublemakers. There is almost always one or two in every league. If they are not checked, fights and other extreme events result – including death. We have all heard and read about such horrible results. They are in the news all too frequently. Too often, ugly things happen because the league didn't have a working policy to purge the WOFATPs.

Leagues run by government entities will have a hard time doing this tough stuff. How can a Government Recreation District tell a taxpayer that they cannot participate? This is another reason why the leagues should be controlled by the parents, not government.

Chapter 16
Balance the Playing Time

Balancing the playing time is critical. The organization must give serious thought to the rules on this crucial subject. Defensive and or offensive plays, innings, periods, at bats, minutes of playing time, or combinations of these or other criteria.

If the teams are made up of two age groups, should the rule be the same for first year and second year kids? The kid who sticks with the program for a second year will likely get some more playing time in the second year just because they have matured and improved. Do we expect approximately equal time? Can the method be easily measured by the team scorekeeper? Consider how to monitor the results – honor system, turn in timesheets, have a league official attend random games, etc. How will you handle disputes between coaches?

Nothing can sour kids and parents more than the perception that they are being "cheated" on playing time. **Establishment of minimum playing time rules will go a long way toward keeping all parents and kids happy without destroying the competition.** This is a giant step toward "parity".

Whatever rules are developed should, in my opinion, be good for the regular season and for playoffs. Changing rules for the playoffs sends a poor message to coaches, players and parents. During the regular season we were interested in parity, now we are interested in winning at all costs. Some would say that "competitive leagues shouldn't have such rules." I would disagree.

At these young ages, even competitive leagues should guarantee a minimum amount of playing time.

After all, according to one study only 0.8% of kids will play college sports and less than 4% of the college players will ever play pro.

At these young ages, kids shouldn't be pushed into a particular sport or pushed to play entire games or be made a pawn in the process. Many studies have proven that playing time at very young ages makes no difference in their ability to excel at older ages. I would contend that how much fun young kids have is far more important to their progress than early age playing time.

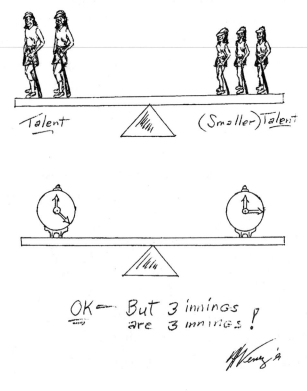

Talent   (Smaller) Talent

OK ← But 3 innings are 3 innings!

Chapter 17
Balance the Talent

Balancing the talent among the teams in the league is critical. When all is said and done this aspect of the league organization is the most important and the most difficult to achieve. Often the person that does the organizing is also a coach. He or she may feel it is their reward for doing all the organization work to get the pick of the talent. No surprise that they win the award for most outhouses tipped. **The sandlot method is the best method going for balancing the talent - a fair draft system.**

One year, a neighbor Gene and I decided to co-coach a girl's softball team. Each team was to carry fifteen girls. The league had carry-over teams with girls on them from last year. The most "carry-overs" on any of the "old" teams was eight. Tryouts were held for all the new girls - Apple Valley Minnesota was growing fast then, so there was a lot of new talent. Each girl was to hit, run the bases, catch and throw. A league organizer pitched to all the girls for consistency.

At the tryouts, Gene and I sat on separate benches and separately rated and ranked all the new girls with a method we had worked out ahead of time. A "draft" was then held to fill each team with fifteen girls. Since we were a brand new team, we were given eight draft picks to "fill our team to the "base of eight". Thus, we and the other new team had the opportunity to pick the best sixteen players – eight each – in turn. Then all teams joined the draft according to the number of carryovers they had.

The other coaches seemed to be more interested in who their daughter wanted on the team or who lived in their neighborhood. They didn't use a rating and ranking method. We therefore drafted not just eight but thirteen of the most talented girls for our team. Since our own daughters were among the best in the league, we had a very powerful team. It was the only back to back undefeated seasons in my coaching career. We had lots of fun but the other teams didn't seem to enjoy it as much as we did.

Is it OK to have such lop-sided results? Was that the best thing for the girls on all the teams? The other coaches were certainly very unhappy with our dominance. What went wrong here? The talent was nowhere near balanced.

In my opinion, the coach should have their own kid(s) on his/her team. After that, what do we do? Organize by neighborhood and hope that the talent is randomly distributed between neighborhoods? If the neighborhoods have about the same player population, this can work. If the schools are running the show, the talent will be distributed according to the school size. If the schools in the league are about the same size, the talent will be fairly evenly distributed. If they aren't, the biggest school is probably going to tip the most outhouses.

But what method is best for an association? **The best method I have seen work well is the universal try-out method.** This method has a tryout, ranking and draft that went something like this.

- All the players, new and "old", would be put through the same drill(s).

- Two or more coaches would grade each and every player – whether they are on an existing team or not.

- The ranking would be summarized by one method – say one to ten for each drill. Then totaled.

- Then the draft would take place by ranking of the players. That is, any team that doesn't have a number one ranked player would draft one such player. Then the number two ranked players, etc.

- Each coach might be given one "personal draft" to get their kid's best friend on their team.

Of course this takes considerable planning for a one time event. Not withstanding the problems associated (what about kids that can't make the tryout, which coaches to use, etc) it is a very good method. Some equitable method must be found because **balancing the talent is the second giant step toward "parity".**

Chapter 18
Drop-Outs

Kid-drop-outs need to be carefully monitored by the league. The league needs to be very diligent in watching coaches who always have one or more kids drop-out for no apparent reason. They are probably the "win at all costs" types. Unfortunately, especially when the league has playing time rules, it isn't beneath those few coaches to find ways to drive off the low talent kids. There are more ways than outhouse designs.

Absolutely the worst example of this kind of coach was recently covered in a Sports Illustrated article. When coaching 8 and 9 year olds, a baseball coach told the parents about the play-off schedule but suggested to them that no one tell the parents of a handicapped kid on the team. League rules called for every kid to play three innings. When the kid showed up anyway, coach offered to pay one of his kids $25 to hit the handicapped kid in warm-ups. When one shot in the groin didn't do the job, coach told the pitcher to "go out there and hit him harder." The next shot in the face and ear properly put the coach in court. Turns out the coach was also facing charges for assaulting his fiancée. This WOFATP (Waste Of Food And Toilet Paper) belongs in jail and certainly out of coaching forever.

The coaches should be required to report each and every drop-out promptly. The league should ask the coach, "Why?" Then check it out. Someone in that organization needs to call the parent, question him / her and talk to the kid if the parent agrees. Talk to another parent or two from that team. Ask some piercing questions. Was their kid treated differently than others? If a coach seems to have "driven off" a low skill kid, the league officials must talk to the coach and let them know, in no uncertain terms, that it is unacceptable. A one-strike card for the coach is in order. This won't have to be done very often as the word will get around.

Are children that move into the league during the season going to be put on a team? If so, they need to be ranked and placed on team that had a drop-out of the same rank. **The league should have a meaningful policy about drop-outs and it should be written and reviewed with the coaches before the season starts.**

Chapter 19
Competitive or Non-competitive

The "competitive vs non-competitive" issue is the hottest one in the outhouse tipping park. What does it mean to be non-competitive? Does it mean that we just don't keep score or is there more to it? Can't we just have fun? We just need to be nice to everyone. We will tell all the kids to "just get along" – not very realistic - especially in football or hockey!

An absence of score keeping works well until about age seven. In T-Ball for five and six year olds, the non-competitive rules (for example; everybody bats every inning and the last person up gets a base clearing hit) do work. Similar methods for other sports at that age may work. Beyond that age however, what can be done? You either have to drastically change the rules of the game or live with the natural competitiveness of kids. Face it, life is competitive. Life isn't fair either. However, the league should constantly strive to make the league as fair as possible.

The "Traveling Team" or "Competitive Team" approach is commonly found. This assumes that there are enough kids in the league to make at least one traveling team. The best kids in the league are offered a chance to compete with the best from other leagues. Voluntary tryouts are usually used to sort out the best. Often, traveling teams are set up without any intention of balancing the playing time. There should still be inter-league rules to balance the playing time. Again, not necessarily equal time but a minimum playing time rule. Imagine how a parent would feel if their kid was selected for an all-star team and didn't play, or played only a token amount.

Does this mean that the kids who are in the rest of the league are non-competitive? We could call them that if it makes some folks feel better, but who are we kidding? "Non-competitive" in sports is an oxymoron. A wish masquerading as a policy! If the government operates the league, they would likely call it a "Feel good, non-competitive, politically-correct, get-along-nicely league." **Denial of competitiveness in Americans is like denial of the urge to tip an outhouse. "Traveling" and "In-house" are more meaningful terms.**

Chapter 20
Plan & Communicate

Needless to say, the league officials must obtain facilities for games and sometimes for practices. This is a difficult process which I have never been part of. They typically do a very good job with it. Most leagues do a pretty fair job at publishing the schedule for the season. The schedule should be handed to all parents via the coach. It is an excellent idea to occasionally print a newsletter. The best organized league I witnessed was in Apple Valley Minnesota kid's hockey. The following newsletter came out in April:

Next Season Notes:
- Registration will be in September – time and dates to be announced.
- Education Week Clinics are planned to be on Oct 19, 20, 21 & 22.
- Traveling Team tryouts - week of October 23 with team selection by Oct 29. Practices will start the next day.
- In-House tryouts will be in mid November.
- Teams selected by early December.
- Indoor practices during December.
- League play to start Christmas week.
- The Big Apple Tournament will be Jan 18, 19, 20 & 21

That is what you call planning ahead. Clinics were held for coaches and kids and the in-house tryouts were for balancing the talent. These folks were extremely well organized and the results showed. The kids that went through that program progressed with superior speed. The ultimate result was a Minnesota State High School Hockey Championship for Apple Valley High School. I was very proud to coach kids in the program who were part of their success.

Chapter 21
Schools and Kids Sports

Outhouse-tippers know that organizing sports in schools is a natural. Government schools, however, seem to want to drop sports - often physical education all together. Amanda Spake wrote in US News; "Now only 8% of elementary schools and 5.8% of high schools offer daily PE in all grades." Disgusting but true. This is why recreation districts have grown so fast.

Modern schools are so big, few students make the sports teams. The result - overweight and out of condition kids. No wonder some teachers want to drug the boys. They are loaded with pent up energy. This is a condition that doesn't match the wishes of 81.4% of the parents per the latest outhouse owner's survey. Some government schools have even tried to prevent the neighborhood association or recreation district from using the school facilities.

Schools are a perfect place to organize sports for kids. Kids need a break from class time and need to work off some of that energy. Physical education for all kids should be mandatory. After hours sports, in lieu of physical education, should be offered for those kids/parents who wish to participate. They are at school. Why bus/drive them elsewhere to play? The outhouse is right there – let's tip it!

Schools that have organized sports should have a "No Pass – No Play" rule including every subject. In fact, considering the grade inflation that is prevalent in most schools, I would readily endorse a requirement of a "C" grade or higher. Let the kids know that school work is more important than sports – period.

Even when the school is organizing a sport, parents should be expected to help out. Parents are much more likely to do what is best for the kids than the government ("public" school is government school). Oh, but the parents don't have time, say the administrators and teachers. Last time I checked, there were lots of parents who would volunteer if they were asked. The typical "cop out" from some teachers, administrators and unions is that the "parents aren't involved." Have the parents been asked? Has anyone called the parents? Have they sent a note home with the kids? Has anyone put an article in the local paper asking parents to volunteer?

The primary and middle schools once had money enough to offer physical education and sports. What has happened? Do you remember voting to eliminate sports and physical education from schools? Could it be that the clique of administrators, school boards and teacher unions played the Washington Monument Closing Game? They say with an almost imperceptible whine, "We don't have enough budget to do what needs to be done so we will have to cut the sports, physical education, band, or whatever."

The tax dollars per student have increased 62.7% faster than the rate of inflation. (That according to a Biffy-Tippers of America study.) The students per classroom are the same or lower then when I went to school. But they don't like to address facts. "Well, our job is teaching, not sports." Are there no lessons to be learned through sports? Can't one learn to "feel good" about themselves in sports as well as in the class room? Won't involvement in sports make better students? Is some of the violence associated with the modern government school occurring because the kids aren't physically challenged?

Chapter 22
Recreation Districts & Kids Sports

Recreation Districts (read Government Tax Districts) have been created to fill the gap left by the schools and working parents. Generally they do a very credible job. However, Rec Districts tend to build an empire by offering something for everyone. After they read this book they will offer a course on outhouse tipping.

District offerings done with volunteer leadership - coaching in our discussion - is the best approach. *If parents don't volunteer, then the activity simply shouldn't be offered. If parents don't care enough to volunteer in order to implement and maintain the activity, then the activity isn't needed.* **This is the "outhouse test" of the worthiness of any recreational activity to be paid with tax dollars.**

"But some of we parents are willing to pay a fee for their kids." So what? The outhouse tipping course is 90% paid by taxes and the parents are willing to pay 10%. Wow! That's a generous portion isn't it? If parents aren't willing to volunteer to implement and maintain the activity then they are simply looking for the rest of the taxpayers to baby sit their kids.

Government recreation districts have no incentive to apply outhouse rules. They, in fact, have incentive to grow their jobs as taxes and fees allow. They also have no incentive to involve parents.

They would prefer to hire coaches. I'm sorry folks, but it's just the facts.

This doesn't mean that the people involved are bad people. On the contrary, they are typically very caring and concerned folks. They like kids and do a very good job for the circumstances they are in.

See that "form"? - Talk about your great Coaching!"

Chapter 23
Rewards and Beginning

In short, you can and should coach kids or help the coach or the organization. Do it. Go for it. You will get more out of it than you put in. The rewards are endless. Coaching my own and other kids gave me rewards throughout my life. I have a jacket that the kids (parents) bought me and presented at our year end party. It is one of my most precious possessions. I also still keep a set of thank-you notes / drawings / poems from kids on my teams. It is special when my own kids tell me that they really appreciated my taking time with their teams. There aren't financial rewards however. If I'd put the hours coaching into earning and investing, I'd probably be considerably dollar-richer today.

I played men's and old timer's hockey until about age 55 and coached kids hockey many of those years. My kids watched, played on my teams and later played with me. I never realized what it meant to my kids until my youngest sent me an article from the ESPN web-site about kids watching their professional dads compete. My son wrote, "I thought the article was great. He (the author) only missed one point. He kept stressing how it was extra cool for these kids because their dad plays in the NHL. I don't think it matters to young kids, NHL or old timers, it was just cool to see your dad competing and setting a positive example. Heck, that you played with my Jr. High gym teacher was just as impressive to me as if you'd played with Gordie Howe."

The primary reward for you will be to know that you have enriched the life of a kid and taught them something about a sport that you like. Your kids and the other kids you coach aren't very likely to become superstars or even continue to play the sport. However, they are very likely to become a fan of the game, a better person, a better worker, a better boss or even a better politician.

When they see you in later years and tell you that they really had fun playing for you, you'll know that you succeeded. One of my sons became a sportscaster and sports talk show host. He probably wouldn't admit that the old man was an influence in that career choice but some things just don't have to be spoken. He still plays and loves sports that I coached him in. My daughter has coached kids soccer and I see some of the old man's teaching coming through. My other son coaches his and other kids in a couple of sports.

It's reward enough to have a child you coached see you on the street or in the grocery store and smile and say, "Hi Coach!"

Can we combine the best of the sand-lot with organized youth sports? Can some sand lot culture be used in competitive leagues? Can we combine the best of sandlot, organization and competition? Can the kids, parents and coaches on both sides feel like winners? This book may not have answered all these questions but hopefully it has made you think about what is best for the children. Not what is best for the parents, not best for the teachers, not best for the city, not best for the coaches, not best for the administrators, not best for the school board, not best for the recreation district, but what is best for the kids. You are the right person to answer these questions. **So if you want to coach, help, or organize, do it! Go for it. It is very likely best for the kids.**

About the Author

The author was raised outside a small country town. Sports were a way of life in the country before TV. So was outhouse tipping – a challenging sport although not too modern. He has tipped more backhouses than 99.6 percent of the population. He gained considerable "wisdom" from this value adding endeavor and applies that wisdom to coaching kids. His other accomplishments include:

- More slivers from bench-warming (another phrase that comes from the outhouse) in his playing days than 92.6% of the population.
- Played many different sports when a kid - sand-lot baseball, football, basketball, golf, speed-skating, pond-hockey, boxing, skiing, diving, swimming and biffy-tipping.
- Purchased a life insurance policy from his high school basketball coach.
- Played several organized sports up through high school. Was asked to try-out for the University of Illinois fencing team by an ex-Olympian, then U of I coach.
- Was the oldest guy on his men's hockey team.
- Was part of a college swim-team that won the university intramural championship.
- Was a starter on his high school baseball team. Of course there were only about a dozen players out for the team. Luckily it was a small school or there would have been more slivers.
- Fought on American Legion and high school boxing teams. Sixty-eight thru one hundred twenty-eight pound classes. More wins than losses. Sixteen ounce gloves prevented brain damage – or did they?

- Once beat the west-coast senior men's ping pong champion sitting down. It was in a high school program – we had a school playoff to determine the best players to take part in the program. This biffy-tipper and three of his best friends won the tournament. They played a lot in their basements in bad weather. By the way . . . **he** was sitting down. He had to be sitting on a milk-stool before hitting the ball.
- Got a concussion practicing high school football.
- Lettered in high school baseball and basketball.
- Played men's baseball, softball, basketball and ice hockey.
- Coached kids for about twenty-six kid-seasons in several sports – boys and girls. Coached boys hockey, girls hockey, boys tee-ball, boys baseball, girls softball and girls soccer. Helped one season with a boys basketball team and another with a track team.
- Coached skiing for handicapped kids for five seasons. Or, more correctly, they taught him how to teach skiing to kids.

About The Artist

Howard Venezia is an extraordinary person and talent. He is not only an expressive artist but a woodcarver and storyteller. He served his country for 36 years in the Navy where he worked his way up the Navy chain of command from Seaman Recruit to Captain (equivalent to a Bird Colonel in the Army), commanding a squadron of ships. A true seaman, Howie bracketed his navy career by serving some 10 years in the Merchant Marine, first in the engineering area and, rounding out that second career, as a licensed Master Mariner.

The author thanks Howie for his time, creativity, artistic and other contributions to this work.

Send your kid-coaching stories
or comments to the author at:

Email: ec3corp@rkymtnhi.com

Or to the publisher via Web Site: www.ecm5tools.com

Or via Snail Mail:
EC3 Corp
P O Box 205
Winter Park, CO 80482

$ 8.00 - Includes Shipping & Handling:
Quantity discounts available.

If you wish the book(s) autographed at no extra charge
(it adds $ .03 to the value but not the price),
include the names for whom the books are intended.